Christopher Columbus

by David Goodnough
illustrated by Burt Dodson

Troll Associates

Troll Associates
Library of Congress Catalog Card Number: 78-18052
ISBN 0-89375-170-7
ISBN 0-89375-162-6 Paper Edition

10   9   8   7   6   5

Christopher Columbus

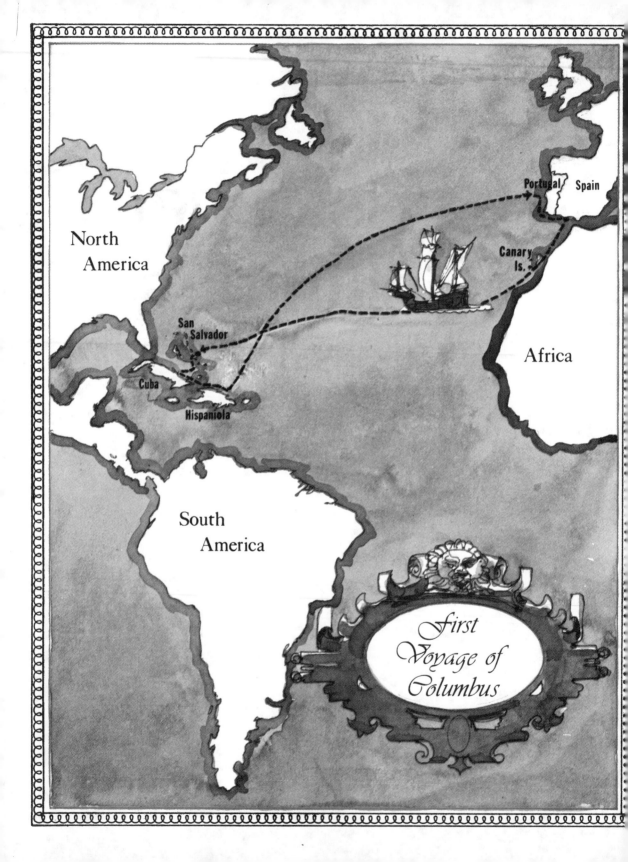

North America

South America

Africa

Portugal   Spain

Canary Is.

San Salvador

Cuba

Hispaniola

First Voyage of Columbus

Young Christopher Columbus was an obedient son. His father was a weaver in the busy city of Genoa, and Christopher worked long hours at the looms. There he wove cloth from the wool that he and his brother had cleaned. The work was dull. The only relief the boy had was when he helped his father deliver the finished cloth to customers in other cities. The roads of northern Italy were bad, so they traveled mostly by sea. This was what Columbus loved.

The bustling port of Genoa always excited Columbus. From the window of his father's house, he could see the ships in the harbor. The cries of the gulls and the sound of hammering and sawing from the shipyards reached him as he toiled at the looms. He longed to escape, and he vowed to himself that as soon as he was old enough, he would go to sea.

By the time Columbus was in his early twenties, he was spending more time at sea than at his father's looms. He had made voyages across the Mediterranean Sea to North Africa, and had traveled to Greece and Portugal as well.

During these early voyages, Columbus worked as a sailor and learned the basics of seamanship. He became used to the long hours on watch, sometimes spent in pouring rain or a howling gale. He took his turn at the tiller and learned how to steer a ship almost by touch. He scrambled high into the rigging to roll up the sails. And he knew the excitement of sighting land on a strange coast after days of seeing nothing but water, sky, and clouds.

6

The only thing that kept Columbus from becoming a master mariner and captain of his own ship was that he did not know how to read and write. This was not unusual in those days. Most people did not know how to read and write—but it kept Columbus from learning how to navigate a ship.

In 1476, something happened that changed the life of Christopher Columbus. He was sailing with a fleet on its way to trade in northern Europe. The ships passed easily through the Strait of Gibraltar and then set their course to the north. But off the coast of Portugal, they met a fleet of enemy warships. There was a battle, and Columbus' ship was hit.

Columbus was slightly wounded, but he was able
to jump overboard before his ship sank. He
grabbed a floating timber, and used it to reach the
shore, six miles away.

The Portuguese people were friendly. They
helped him get to the capital city of Lisbon, where
his brother Bartholomew worked as a chart-
maker. It was here in Lisbon that Columbus got
the chance to complete his education.

At that time, Portugal was one of the greatest seafaring countries in the world. The king wanted to trade with other countries outside the Mediterranean Sea. Portuguese mariners had already begun to explore the coast of Africa.

Portugal had become a center of learning for mariners—a place where all information about the sea and seamanship could be exchanged. Here, Columbus could learn all he needed to know to become a master mariner.

He was a remarkable student. Soon he was reading and writing in Latin, Portuguese, and Spanish. He also learned mathematics and—most important—navigation.

Columbus was fascinated by the writings of the ancient geographers, and by Marco Polo's accounts of his journey to Asia in 1271. Columbus dreamed of the day he would command his own ship and lead great voyages of discovery.

By the 1400's, most educated people knew that the earth was round. But they thought the earth included only the continents of Europe, Africa, and Asia—and one great "Ocean Sea."

12

Many people were excited by the idea that Asia—which Europeans called the *Indies*—could be reached by sea. They did not know where the African continent ended. But there was talk that, by sailing around Africa and then eastward, it would be an easy matter to reach Asia. Here, they were sure, treasures of gold, jewels, silk, and spices awaited them.

13

By 1478, Columbus was a master mariner. Now he often served as captain on the ships he sailed. He had married, and he and his wife lived in the Madeira Islands, where their son Diego was born. His wife's father had been a sea captain and explorer, and Columbus inherited all his maps, logbooks, and navigational instruments.

As time passed, Columbus became more and more convinced that the eastern sea route was *not* the shortest and easiest way to reach the Indies. He believed that the quickest and most direct route to Asia was *west*—across the unknown waters of what sailors called the Sea of Darkness.

Columbus calculated that the distance from the Canary Islands off the coast of Africa to the island of Japan was only 2,400 nautical miles. This was a huge error. The actual distance is over 10,000 nautical miles. But Columbus was convinced he was right.

Columbus was not the only man who believed that the ocean between Europe and Asia was narrow. He corresponded with a famous Italian astronomer named Toscanelli. The astronomer congratulated Columbus for his "great and noble ambition to pass over to where the spices grow." Toscanelli agreed that the western sea route to Asia could easily be navigated.

16

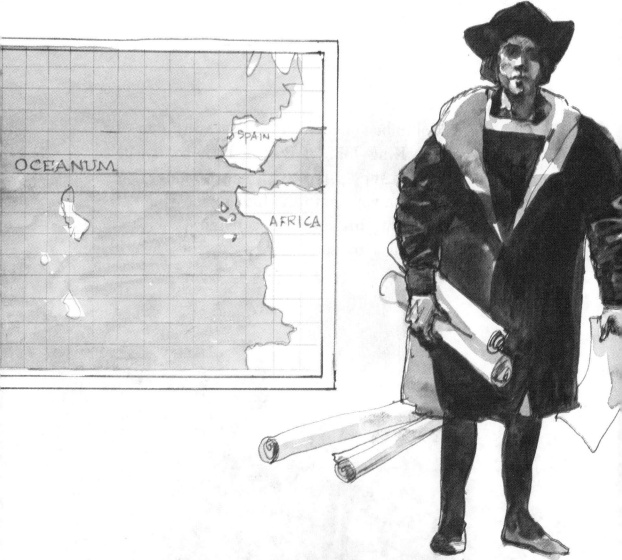

Armed with letters and encouragement, Columbus was ready to reveal his plan to the world. He would sail west to Asia. And he would become rich and famous for fulfilling such a noble mission!

In 1484, Columbus managed to get an appointment with King John of Portugal. He boldly asked the king to supply him with ships, money, and men to make a voyage to the Indies. The king was interested. But his advisors convinced him that Columbus' idea of sailing west to find the East was foolish.

Now there was nothing left in Portugal for Columbus. His wife had died. His brother Bartholomew had gone to get help from England and France for the voyage. And so, Columbus decided to seek help in Spain.

With his young son Diego, Columbus traveled to Palos, just across the border in Spain. There he placed Diego at the monastery of La Rábida, where the monks had a boarding school.

Columbus now met an important monk—one who had influence at the Spanish court. The monk listened to Columbus' ideas with great interest. Eventually, he arranged for Columbus to meet the king and queen of Spain.

At their first meeting, Queen Isabella was very impressed with Columbus. He spoke well, and his eyes shone with excitement as he explained his plan to reach the Indies. But in spite of this, King Ferdinand and Queen Isabella did not want to act too quickly. They were deeply involved in an expensive war with the Moors.

20

Finally, they decided to turn the matter over to their advisors. And for several years, no decision was made. Columbus followed the court of the king and queen all over Spain. He was so sure his plan was a good one that he never lost hope. He firmly believed that, sooner or later, he would get his ships and sail to the Indies. Finally, the royal advisors made their report. "Your Royal Majesties," they said, "the ocean is much larger than Columbus believes. It would not be wise to invest in this voyage."

Columbus' plan seemed doomed. But he would not let this stop him. He was still sure it was his destiny to find the western sea route to Asia. He would look for help elsewhere. Columbus now decided to join his brother in France.

But Queen Isabella could not forget what Columbus had said. She thought of the wealth and glory that would come to Spain if his daring plan succeeded. Then, just before Columbus left for France, Isabella called him back to court. She had decided not to take the advice of the experts.

"You shall have my help in your voyage," she said. "If necessary, I shall sell my crown jewels to raise the money for your brave venture!"

Columbus was overjoyed. But now he made some strong demands. He wanted the title of Admiral, along with ships and men. He also wanted to be made governor and ruler of any new lands he discovered and to share in any profits made from trade with these lands. Isabella was astounded.

"You are an ungrateful fool to ask so much. These are outrageous demands!" she declared. Then she dismissed Columbus from her court. Once again, Columbus prepared to leave. He was ready to start all over again at the court of the French king. But at the last minute, Isabella sent for Columbus. She agreed to all of his demands.

Columbus decided to prepare for his voyage at Palos. He was now well known in Spain, and had made friends with a famous shipbuilding family named Pinzón. Two of the Pinzóns would command two of the three ships in his fleet.

26

Columbus chose a small square-rigged vessel named the *Santa Maria* for his flagship. The Pinzóns provided two smaller vessels called caravels—the *Pinta* and the *Niña*. The ninety men who made up the crews for these ships were from Palos or nearby—and all of them were good sailors.

On August 3, 1492, Columbus boarded the *Santa Maria*. There was no ceremony except prayers and hymns. In the early hours of the morning, the tiny fleet sailed out of the harbor of Palos. Columbus—now an Admiral—commanded confidently from his ship.

His plan was simple. He would proceed to the Canary Islands and then make the long jump to the Indies. He did not know that a whole continent lay in his way.

After a short stay in the Canary Islands for repairs and supplies, the fleet headed due west. Soon the men on board lost the last sight of land. They were all experienced sailors, but none of them had ever been out of sight of land for more than three weeks. They wondered what adventures were waiting for them.

At first the water was calm and the wind strong and steady. The fleet made good headway. The weather was so fine, in fact, that the captains of the three ships could talk to each other over the open water. Everyone was happy and confident.

But then the weather turned bad. The sailors grew concerned. The shore birds had long since disappeared. Everyone knew they were farther out to sea than anyone had ever been before. Why did they not sight land?

After eight weeks, it was clear to all that they had gone much farther than the 2,400 miles that Columbus had said was the distance between Europe and the Indies. Sailors began to grumble and fight among themselves. There was talk of turning back. Columbus dealt quickly with this. He spurred the men on, saying, "We have sailed to find the Indies, and we shall not turn back." "Sail on!" shouted one of his captains in support.

Then one day birds began to appear in the sky. Floating branches bobbed alongside the ships. There were clouds on the horizon. The sailors knew from these signs that they were near land. Now they began to have more trust in Columbus. None of the sailors had ever thought they would fall off the edge of the world, or be devoured by sea monsters. Still . . . they had wondered what would become of them.

Excitement was high. Columbus offered a reward to the first sailor who sighted land. There were some false alarms. Then, on the night of October 11, Columbus and a crew member thought they saw a light in the darkness.

Every man on watch strained to see, hear, or even smell the land they knew lay ahead.

Suddenly, at two o'clock in the morning of October 12, 1492, a lookout on the *Pinta* shouted, "*Tierra! Tierra!* Land! Land!"

In the moonlight lay the white cliffs of a small island. Columbus immediately ordered his crews to shorten sail. He pulled his small fleet together. This was no time to run aground!

The ships bobbed on the waves until dawn. The sailors were hardly able to control their excitement. Was this the Indies at last? Or was it one of the islands they believed lay in the middle of the Ocean Sea? The night seemed endless. Finally, the sun rose, casting its light on the strange shore.

Columbus directed his ships southward, away from the dangerous cliffs.

Columbus and the Pinzón brothers went ashore in a longboat. When they landed on the white beach, they immediately planted the royal banner of Spain. Everyone in the landing party fell to his knees and offered thanks for their safe arrival. Columbus named the island San Salvador.

Columbus believed that he was on islands just off the shore of China or Japan. Now we know he had landed in the Bahamas, southeast of Florida.

Columbus and his men stayed on San Salvador for only a few days. The people who lived on the island soon appeared, bringing gifts for the strangers who had arrived from nowhere. They were a gentle and peaceful people. Because Columbus believed he was in the Indies, he called them *Indians*.

The Spaniards noticed that many of the Indians wore ornaments made of gold. Using sign language, the Indians told Columbus there were many more islands to the south and north, from where the gold had come. Columbus wanted to return to Spain with something of value to present to the king and queen, so he set sail in quest of gold.

Indian guides directed Columbus south through a chain of islands. Everywhere Columbus landed, he found the same thing—friendly and cooperative people, but none of the riches and splendor of Japan and China. The Indians indicated that there was a large island farther south, where there was much gold to be found. This island was Cuba, but Columbus believed it was either Japan or the eastern tip of China.

For several days, Columbus explored the northern coast of Cuba. But still he found no gold. He sent scouting parties inland to look for great cities and golden palaces, but they found only friendly Indians and small villages. Again, the Indians told of another large island to the east, rich in gold.

Columbus made the short voyage across what is now called the Windward Passage. He soon sighted the most beautiful land he had ever seen. It was Haiti. He named the entire island Hispaniola—the "Spanish Island."

The Indians on Hispaniola seemed to have plenty of gold. And they willingly traded it or gave it to the Spaniards. When a powerful chief on the north coast of Hispaniola invited Columbus to visit him, Columbus quickly set sail. He believed that great gold mines were located in this area.

41

For once, Columbus let his guard down. On Christmas Eve, 1492, the entire watch on the *Santa Maria* was asleep. They were exhausted from the farewell celebration the Indians had given them. The tiller was in the hands of a small boy. The *Santa Maria* quietly ran onto a coral reef, which pierced holes in her bottom.

Columbus knew he could not save his ship. But he believed this was a sign that a colony should be built here for Spain. Most of the crew members jumped at the chance to stay in this land filled with gold. They happily set about building a fort out of the *Santa Maria*'s timbers and plankings.

Columbus was now ready to return to Spain and report to the king and queen. He set sail on the *Niña* in early January, 1493. But the return voyage of the ships was rough and difficult. Finally, on March 3, he managed to bring the *Niña* into the harbor at Lisbon, Portugal.

Columbus was anxious to announce his success to the king and queen of Spain. So he set off around the coast of Portugal. And on March 15, 1493, he arrived at Palos, Spain.

Ferdinand and Isabella were overjoyed at the news of his return. They quickly sent a message addressing Columbus as "Admiral of the Ocean Sea, Viceroy and Governor of the Islands that he hath discovered in the Indies." Thus ended happily one of the greatest adventures of all time—the first voyage of Christopher Columbus.

Columbus would make three more voyages to what he still thought were the Indies. He would discover all of the large islands of the Caribbean Sea, and he would touch on the South American continent, Central America, and the Isthmus of Panama. The only thing he would miss would be the large continent to the north.

The colony Columbus had founded on his first voyage was wiped out by unfriendly Indians who had been offended by the Spaniards' greed for gold. But on his second voyage, Columbus began a permanent colony on Hispaniola. The colony prospered and became the base for all future Spanish exploration in the New World.

Unfortunately, Columbus' fame and fortune did not last. After his fourth voyage, which lasted from 1502 until 1504, he was ignored by the court and government officials. Many were jealous of his successes. Others believed he was an impractical dreamer, unfit to govern the lands he had discovered.

Columbus spent the rest of his life following the court from city to city, pleading for his rights. Even though his discoveries had made him a fairly rich man, Columbus was not satisfied without the recognition and honors he believed Spain owed him.

When Queen Isabella died, King Ferdinand lost all interest in him. Sick and frustrated, Christopher Columbus died on May 20, 1506, while planning another voyage to the Indies.

Columbus died almost alone, still believing that he had discovered islands off the coast of Asia. He did not realize that he had made the greatest discovery of all. He had opened the door to a vast New World.